Here is an example to use this journal

Day 1

Today I am MOST grateful for:

My brand new Gratitude Journal!

Because:

Learning to be grateful is VERY IMPORTANT. It will help me make the most of my life and be HAPPY :)

More reasons to feel happy about today:

The sun is shining!
I scored an "A" on my math test.
Our team won the match :)
Yummy chocolate Ice-cream for desert! :)

Fill out just one page every day. It only takes a few minutes. I promise you will be VERY glad that you did.

Day 1

Today I am MOST grateful for:

_____
_____

Because:

_____
_____
_____

More reasons to feel happy about today:

_____
_____
_____
_____

Day 2

Today I am MOST grateful for:

_____

_____

Because:

_____

_____

More reasons to feel happy about today:

_____

_____

_____

_____

Day 3

Today I am MOST grateful for:

_____

_____

Because:

_____

_____

_____

More reasons to feel happy about today:

_____

_____

_____

_____

_____

Day 4

Today I am MOST grateful for:

_____

Because:

_____
_____

More reasons to feel happy about today:

_____
_____
_____

Day 5

Today I am MOST grateful for:

_____
_____

Because:

_____
_____
_____

More reasons to feel happy about today:

_____
_____
_____
_____

Day 6

Today I am MOST grateful for:

_____

_____

Because:

_____

_____

More reasons to feel happy about today:

_____

_____

_____

_____

Day 7

Today I am MOST grateful for:

_____
_____

Because:

_____
_____
_____

More reasons to feel happy about today:

_____
_____
_____
_____
_____

Day 8

Today I am MOST grateful for:

_____

_____

Because:

_____

_____

More reasons to feel happy about today:

_____

_____

_____

_____

Day 9

Today I am MOST grateful for:

_____
_____

Because:

_____
_____
_____

More reasons to feel happy about today:

_____
_____
_____
_____
_____

Day 10

Today I am MOST grateful for:

_____
_____

Because:

_____
_____
_____

More reasons to feel happy about today:

_____
_____
_____
_____
_____

Day 11

Today I am MOST grateful for:

_____
_____

Because:

_____
_____
_____

More reasons to feel happy about today:

_____
_____
_____
_____

Day 12

Today I am MOST grateful for:

_____
_____

Because:

_____
_____

More reasons to feel happy about today:

_____
_____
_____
_____

Day 13

Today I am MOST grateful for:

_____
_____

Because:

_____
_____
_____

More reasons to feel happy about today:

_____
_____
_____
_____

Day 14

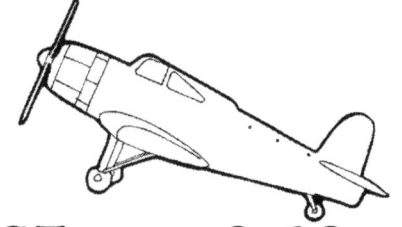

Today I am MOST grateful for:

_____
_____

Because:

_____
_____

More reasons to feel happy about today:

_____
_____
_____
_____

Day 15

Today I am MOST grateful for:

_____
_____

Because:

_____
_____

More reasons to feel happy about today:

_____
_____
_____

Day 16

Today I am MOST grateful for:

_____

Because:

_____
_____

More reasons to feel happy about today:

_____
_____
_____
_____

Day 17

Today I am MOST grateful for:

_____
_____

Because:

_____
_____

More reasons to feel happy about today:

_____
_____
_____
_____

Day 18

Today I am MOST grateful for:

_____
_____

Because:

_____
_____

More reasons to feel happy about today:

_____
_____
_____
_____

Day 19

Today I am MOST grateful for:

_____
_____

Because:

_____
_____
_____

More reasons to feel happy about today:

_____
_____
_____
_____

Day 20

Today I am MOST grateful for:

_____
_____

Because:

_____
_____
_____

More reasons to feel happy about today:

_____
_____
_____
_____

Day 21

Today I am MOST grateful for:

_____

_____

Because:

_____

_____

More reasons to feel happy about today:

_____

_____

_____

_____

Day 22

Today I am MOST grateful for:

_____

_____

Because:

_____

_____

More reasons to feel happy about today:

_____

_____

_____

_____

Day 23

Today I am MOST grateful for:

_____
_____

Because:

_____
_____
_____

More reasons to feel happy about today:

_____
_____
_____
_____

Day 24

Today I am MOST grateful for:

_____
_____

Because:

_____
_____
_____

More reasons to feel happy about today:

_____
_____
_____
_____

Day 25

Today I am MOST grateful for:

_____
_____

Because:

_____
_____
_____

More reasons to feel happy about today:

_____
_____
_____
_____

Day 26

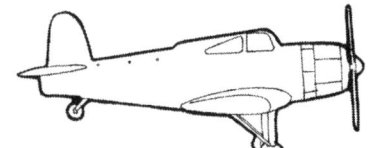

Today I am MOST grateful for:

_____
_____

Because:

_____
_____
_____

More reasons to feel happy about today:

_____
_____
_____
_____

Day 27

Today I am MOST grateful for:

_____
_____

Because:

_____
_____
_____

More reasons to feel happy about today:

_____
_____
_____
_____

Day 28

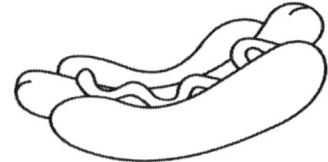

Today I am MOST grateful for:

_____
_____

Because:

_____
_____
_____

More reasons to feel happy about today:

_____
_____
_____
_____

Day 29

Today I am MOST grateful for:

_____
_____

Because:

_____
_____
_____

More reasons to feel happy about today:

_____
_____
_____
_____

Day 30

Today I am MOST grateful for:

_____
_____

Because:

_____
_____
_____

More reasons to feel happy about today:

_____
_____
_____
_____

Day 31

Today I am MOST grateful for:

_____
_____

Because:

_____
_____

More reasons to feel happy about today:

_____
_____
_____
_____

Day 32

Today I am MOST grateful for:

_____
_____

Because:

_____
_____

More reasons to feel happy about today:

_____
_____
_____
_____

Day 33

Today I am MOST grateful for:

_____
_____

Because:

_____
_____

More reasons to feel happy about today:

_____
_____
_____
_____

Day 34

Today I am MOST grateful for:

_____
_____

Because:

_____
_____

More reasons to feel happy about today:

_____
_____
_____
_____

Day 35

Today I am MOST grateful for:

_____

_____

Because:

_____

_____

_____

More reasons to feel happy about today:

_____

_____

_____

_____

Day 36

Today I am MOST grateful for:

_____
_____

Because:

_____
_____

More reasons to feel happy about today:

_____
_____
_____
_____

Day 37

Today I am MOST grateful for:

_____
_____

Because:

_____
_____

More reasons to feel happy about today:

_____
_____
_____
_____

Day 38

Today I am MOST grateful for:

_____
_____

Because:

_____
_____

More reasons to feel happy about today:

_____
_____
_____
_____

Day 39

Today I am MOST grateful for:

_____
_____

Because:

_____
_____
_____

More reasons to feel happy about today:

_____
_____
_____
_____

Day 40

Today I am MOST grateful for:

_____
_____

Because:

_____
_____
_____

More reasons to feel happy about today:

_____
_____
_____
_____

Day 41

Today I am MOST grateful for:

_____
_____

Because:

_____
_____

More reasons to feel happy about today:

_____
_____
_____
_____

Day 42

Today I am MOST grateful for:

_____
_____

Because:

_____
_____

More reasons to feel happy about today:

_____
_____
_____
_____

Day 43

Today I am MOST grateful for:

_____
_____

Because:

_____
_____
_____

More reasons to feel happy about today:

_____
_____
_____
_____

Day 44

Today I am MOST grateful for:

_____
_____

Because:

_____
_____
_____

More reasons to feel happy about today:

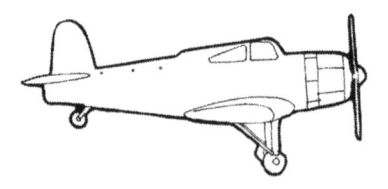

_____
_____
_____
_____

Day 45

Today I am MOST grateful for:

_____
_____

Because:

_____
_____
_____

More reasons to feel happy about today:

_____
_____
_____
_____

Day 46

Today I am MOST grateful for:

_____
_____

Because:

_____
_____

More reasons to feel happy about today:

_____
_____
_____
_____

Day 47

Today I am MOST grateful for:

_____

_____

Because:

_____

_____

More reasons to feel happy about today:

_____

_____

_____

_____

Day 48

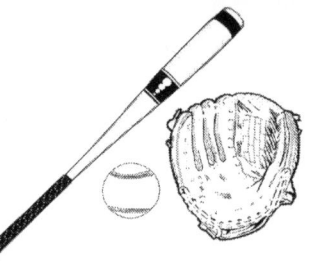

Today I am MOST grateful for:

_____
_____

Because:

_____
_____
_____

More reasons to feel happy about today:

_____
_____
_____
_____

Day 49

Today I am MOST grateful for:

_____
_____

Because:

_____
_____
_____

More reasons to feel happy about today:

_____
_____
_____
_____

Day 50

Today I am MOST grateful for:

_____

_____

Because:

_____

_____

More reasons to feel happy about today:

_____

_____

_____

_____

Day 51

Today I am MOST grateful for:

_____

_____

Because:

_____

_____

_____

More reasons to feel happy about today:

_____

_____

_____

_____

Day 52

Today I am MOST grateful for:

___

___

Because:

___

___

___

More reasons to feel happy about today:

___

___

___

___

Day 53

Today I am MOST grateful for:

_____

Because:

_____
_____
_____

More reasons to feel happy about today:

_____
_____
_____
_____

Day 54

Today I am MOST grateful for:

_____

_____

Because:

_____

_____

_____

More reasons to feel happy about today:

_____

_____

_____

_____

Day 55

Today I am MOST grateful for:

_____
_____

Because:

_____
_____

More reasons to feel happy about today:

_____
_____
_____
_____

Day 56

Today I am MOST grateful for:

_____
_____

Because:

_____
_____
_____

More reasons to feel happy about today:

_____
_____
_____
_____

Day 57

Today I am MOST grateful for:

_____
_____

Because:

_____
_____
_____

More reasons to feel happy about today:

_____
_____
_____
_____

Day 58

Today I am MOST grateful for:

_____

_____

Because:

_____

_____

More reasons to feel happy about today:

_____

_____

_____

_____

Day 59

Today I am MOST grateful for:

_____

_____

Because:

_____

_____

_____

More reasons to feel happy about today:

_____

_____

_____

_____

_____

Day 60

Today I am MOST grateful for:

_____
_____

Because:

_____
_____
_____

More reasons to feel happy about today:

_____
_____
_____
_____

Day 61

Today I am MOST grateful for:

_____
_____

Because:

_____
_____
_____

More reasons to feel happy about today:

_____
_____
_____
_____

Day 62

Today I am MOST grateful for:

_____

_____

Because:

_____

_____

More reasons to feel happy about today:

_____

_____

_____

_____

Day 63

Today I am MOST grateful for:

_____
_____

Because:

_____
_____

More reasons to feel happy about today:

_____
_____
_____
_____

Day 64

Today I am MOST grateful for:

_____
_____

Because:

_____
_____
_____

More reasons to feel happy about today:

_____
_____
_____
_____

Day 65

Today I am MOST grateful for:

___

___

Because:

___

___

___

More reasons to feel happy about today:

___

___

___

___

Day 66

Today I am MOST grateful for:

_____
_____

Because:

_____
_____
_____

More reasons to feel happy about today:

_____
_____
_____
_____

Day 67

Today I am MOST grateful for:

_____

_____

Because:

_____

_____

More reasons to feel happy about today:

_____

_____

_____

_____

Day 68

Today I am MOST grateful for:

_____

_____

Because:

_____

_____

_____

More reasons to feel happy about today:

_____

_____

_____

_____

Day 69

Today I am MOST grateful for:

_____
_____

Because:

_____
_____

More reasons to feel happy about today:

_____
_____
_____
_____

Day 70

Today I am MOST grateful for:

_____
_____

Because:

_____
_____
_____

More reasons to feel happy about today:

_____
_____
_____
_____

Day 71

Today I am MOST grateful for:

_____
_____

Because:

_____
_____

More reasons to feel happy about today:

_____
_____
_____
_____

Day 72

Today I am MOST grateful for:

_____

Because:

_____
_____
_____

More reasons to feel happy about today:

_____
_____
_____
_____

Day 73

Today I am MOST grateful for:

_____

_____

Because:

_____

_____

_____

More reasons to feel happy about today:

_____

_____

_____

_____

Day 74

Today I am MOST grateful for:

_____
_____

Because:

_____
_____
_____

More reasons to feel happy about today:

_____
_____
_____
_____

Day 75

Today I am MOST grateful for:

_____

Because:

_____
_____

More reasons to feel happy about today:

_____
_____
_____
_____

Day 76

Today I am MOST grateful for:

_____

_____

Because:

_____

_____

More reasons to feel happy about today:

_____

_____

_____

Day 77

Today I am MOST grateful for:

_____
_____

Because:

_____
_____
_____

More reasons to feel happy about today:

_____
_____
_____
_____

Day 78

Today I am MOST grateful for:

_____
_____

Because:

_____
_____
_____

More reasons to feel happy about today:

_____
_____
_____
_____

Day 79

Today I am MOST grateful for:

_____
_____

Because:

_____
_____

More reasons to feel happy about today:

_____
_____
_____
_____

Day 80

Today I am MOST grateful for:

_____

_____

Because:

_____

_____

More reasons to feel happy about today:

_____

_____

_____

_____

Day 81

Today I am MOST grateful for:

_____
_____

Because:

_____
_____

More reasons to feel happy about today:

_____
_____
_____
_____

Day 82

Today I am MOST grateful for:

_____
_____

Because:

_____
_____
_____

More reasons to feel happy about today:

_____
_____
_____
_____

Day 83

Today I am MOST grateful for:

_____
_____

Because:

_____
_____
_____

More reasons to feel happy about today:

_____
_____
_____
_____

Day 84

Today I am MOST grateful for:

_____
_____

Because:

_____
_____

More reasons to feel happy about today:

_____
_____
_____
_____

Day 85

Today I am MOST grateful for:

___

Because:

___
___

More reasons to feel happy about today:

___
___
___
___

Day 86

Today I am MOST grateful for:

_____
_____

Because:

_____
_____
_____

More reasons to feel happy about today:

_____
_____
_____
_____

Day 87

Today I am MOST grateful for:

_____
_____

Because:

_____
_____
_____

More reasons to feel happy about today:

_____
_____
_____
_____

Day 88

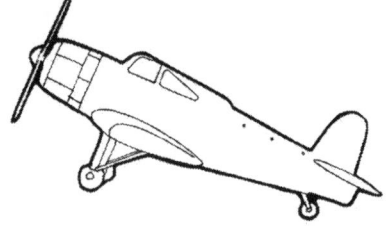

Today I am MOST grateful for:

_____
_____

Because:

_____
_____
_____

More reasons to feel happy about today:

_____
_____
_____
_____

Day 89

Today I am MOST grateful for:

_____
_____

Because:

_____
_____
_____

More reasons to feel happy about today:

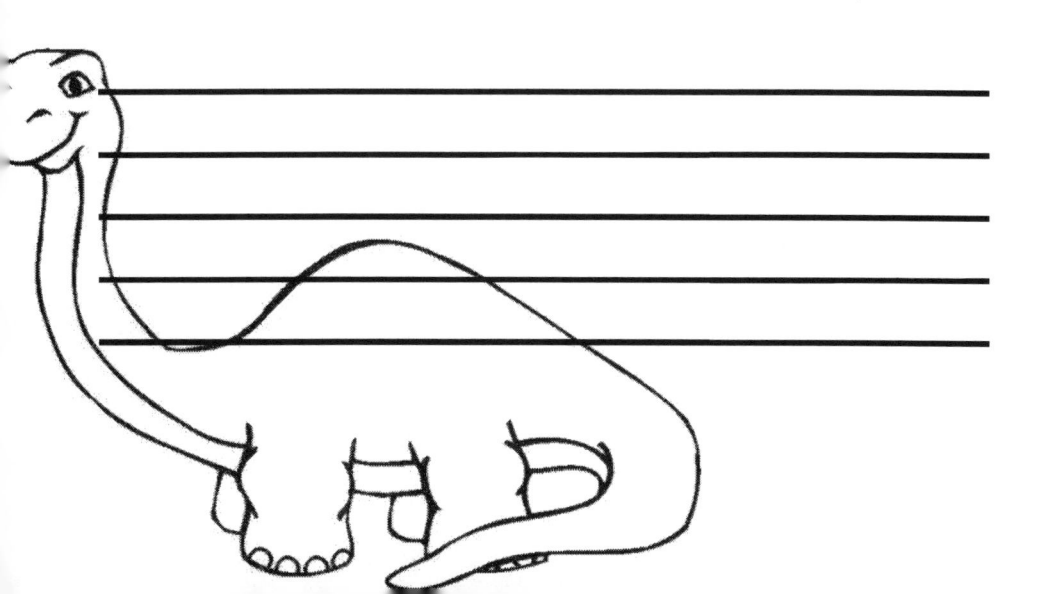

_____
_____
_____
_____
_____

Day 90

Today I am MOST grateful for:

_____

_____

Because:

_____

_____

_____

More reasons to feel happy about today:

_____

_____

_____

_____

Day 91

Today I am MOST grateful for:

_____
_____

Because:

_____
_____

More reasons to feel happy about today:

_____
_____
_____
_____

Day 92

Today I am MOST grateful for:

_____
_____

Because:

_____
_____

More reasons to feel happy about today:

_____
_____
_____
_____

Day 93

Today I am MOST grateful for:

_____
_____

Because:

_____
_____

More reasons to feel happy about today:

_____
_____
_____

Day 94

Today I am MOST grateful for:

_____
_____

Because:

_____
_____
_____

More reasons to feel happy about today:

_____
_____
_____
_____

Day 95

Today I am MOST grateful for:

_____

Because:

_____

_____

More reasons to feel happy about today:

_____

_____

_____

_____

Day 96

Today I am MOST grateful for:

_____
_____

Because:

_____
_____

More reasons to feel happy about today:

_____
_____
_____
_____

Day 97

Today I am MOST grateful for:

_____
_____

Because:

_____
_____

More reasons to feel happy about today:

_____
_____
_____
_____

Day 98

Today I am MOST grateful for:

_____
_____

Because:

_____
_____

More reasons to feel happy about today:

_____
_____
_____
_____

Day 99

Today I am MOST grateful for:

_____
_____

Because:

_____
_____

More reasons to feel happy about today:

_____
_____
_____
_____

Day 100

Today I am MOST grateful for:

_____
_____

Because:

_____
_____
_____

More reasons to feel happy about today:

_____
_____
_____
_____